YOUTH

m☉nday morning™

Movement Time

By Jean Warren
Illustrated by Susan True

Publisher: Roberta Suid
Editor: Bonnie Bernstein
Design: David Hale
Cover art: Corbin Hillam

ISBN 0-912107-17-0

Printed in the United States of America

9 8 7 6 5 4 3 2

PREFACE

As young children grow and develop, they need many opportunities to express themselves. Through open-ended movement activities, children can explore their feelings, interpret visual suggestions, and experiment with their own solutions to hypothetical problems.

Like the other titles in the Play-and-Learn series, **Movement Time** provides parents and teachers with a collection of practical ideas that are developmentally geared to young children. As they participate in the activities, children will discover the relationships between their bodies and the space they move in. They'll practice a variety of movement skills (such as hopping, rolling, and throwing) and explore movement concepts (such as slow, high, and forward).

The activities are designed to exercise the children's imaginations as well as their bodies. Individual ideas are grouped by theme under appropriate seasonal headings. Each group includes a creative warm-up exercise and one or more songs and poems to be accompanied by movements. There might also be a story or imaginative situation for which the children are asked to perform the actions and make up their own endings or solutions. Or there may be an activity that encourages the children to practice observation and coordination skills as they move in ways analagous to animals and things in the world around them, for example, caterpillars or machines.

Adults should be enthusiastic when they are presenting a movement idea to their children, but they should also be prepared to abandon an activity if the children become disinterested. Although some activities are more structured, describing a particular movement or combined movements in detail, most leave the action to the children's willingness and imagination. It's best to let the performers decide which story elements to be acted out and to accept their interpretations, however bizarre. The more freely the children are encouraged to express themselves through their body movements, the more confident they will become in communicating their ideas in general.

The activities in this book were compiled from ideas featured in **Totline**, a 24-page bi-monthly newsletter. The **Totline** regularly features preschool activities in the following areas: art, creative movement, coordination, language development, learning games, science, and self-awareness. Each issue also includes holiday party ideas, sugarless snack recipes, and a special infant-toddler ideas section. For more information, write: Warren Publishing House, P.O. Box 2255, Everett, WA 98203.

CONTENTS

FALL THEMES

Harvesting

Harvesting Hands Warm-Up

Have the children examine their hands and experiment to find different ways to move their hand, fingers, and wrists. When they are standing still, how far out, up, and down can they stretch their hands? How would they use their hands to pick up something heavy, like a pumpkin? Can they lift it over their heads? How would they pick up something slimy, sticky, round? Can they make their hands become gentle hands, rough hands, weak hands, working hands, playful hands?

Harvesting Movements

Lead from the more general hand movements into specific ways that hands can harvest fruits and vegetables. Have the children climb an imaginary ladder and use their hands to pick fruit such as apples, oranges, and cherries. Next have the harvesters dig in the dirt with their hands to gather potatoes and pull carrots. Give each child a turn to name a fruit or vegetable and then have everyone act out how it is harvested.

Vegetable Soup

After the children have harvested all their fruits and vegetables, ask them to help make some vegetable soup. Everyone stands around an imaginary soup pot, stirring as they add the vegetables. Let the children decide which vegetables to add to the pot. As they stir, they can sing the "Vegetable Soup" song.

Song: "Vegetable Soup"

(Sing to the tune of "The Farmer in the Dell.")

The soup is boiling up
The soup is boiling up
Stir slow, around we go
The soup is boiling up.

Other verses:
    First we cook the broth . . .
    Now we add some carrots . . .
    Next we'll add some corn . . .
    Next we'll add some beans...

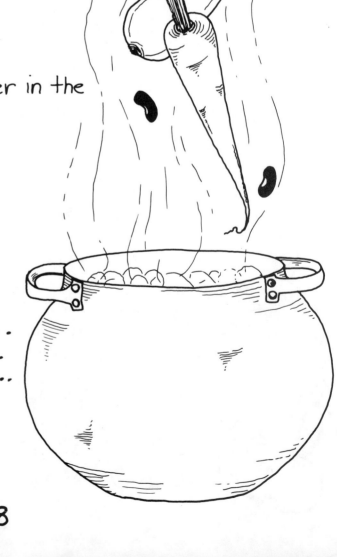

Leaves

Wind Warm-Ups

Have your children imagine that they are beautifully colored autumn leaves swaying in the autumn breeze. Tape long crepe paper streamers to one child's arms so that she becomes the breeze, winding her way through the leaves. The leaves begin to flutter as the wind comes closer. When the breeze is full and hard, the leaves break away from the tree and fall to the ground. Let the children see how many different ways they can fall to the ground—gently floating, spinning, swaying, bouncing, and so on.

Raking Leaves

Next ask your children to pretend that they are out raking the autumn leaves. Have the children rake all the leaves into a large pile. How will the activity end? Let the children decide after you offer these suggestions:

- The children might want to play in the leaves—rolling, sliding, and tossing.
  - Perhaps the wind will pick up again and undo all their hard work. The children can all wear streamers now and be the wind.

continued...

Raking Leaves — *continued*

- The children can stuff the leaves in large bags. The children choose partners. One child is the giant bag, holding his arms in a wide open circle. The other child picks up armfuls of leaves and stuffs them into the "bag."

Song: "Falling Leaves"
(Sing to the tune of "Twinkle, Twinkle, Little Star.")

Chorus: All join hands and circle round
        While we watch the leaves fall down.

See them swirling to the ground
Whirling, twirling all around.
    (chorus)

See them skipping here and there
Dipping, flipping in the air.
    (chorus)

Autumn leaves so peacefully
Falling, falling from the tree.
    (chorus)

Halloween Cat

Cat Warm-Up

Explore the characteristics of cats. Have your children imitate cat movements — how they walk, how they play with a ball of string or curl up in front of a warm fire, how they act when they are angry or afraid. This can all lead into a delightful dramatization about a black cat on Halloween.

Halloween Story

A little black cat is slinking about lost, cold and hungry on a Halloween night. Can your children think of things that would frighten him? Trick-or-treaters dressed as goblins might scare him; so might pumpkins with their glowing grins. The children can act out whatever scary aspects of the drama they wish at this point. You can meanwhile continue the story yourself, telling how a friendly witch finds the lost cat, brings him home, lets him dry out by the fire, feeds him some donuts, and takes him for a ride on her broomstick. Or you can let your children develop and finish the story themselves — it will probably have a more imaginative ending!

Poem: "Black Cat"

Black cat, black cat, turn around.
Black cat, black cat, touch the ground.

Black cat, black cat, jump up high.
Black cat, black cat, touch the sky.

Black cat, black cat, reach down low.
Black cat, black cat, touch your toe.

You and your children can change the
"black cat" to any other Halloween character
— for example, "white ghost," "pumpkin,"
"Ms. Witch," "scarecrow," "Mr. Owl," or
"spider."

Poem: "Wise Owl"

Wise owl, wise owl
Sitting in the tree
Wise owl, wise owl
What do you see?

I see cats
Running by me
All night long
As I sit in my tree.

(Repeat first stanza.)

I see pumpkins
Rolling by me
All night long
As I sit in my tree.

Other possible stanzas:
   I see scarecrows flapping by me...
   I see ghosts floating by me...
   I see witches flying by me...
   I see spiders crawling by me...

Ghosts

Scarf Warm-Up
Show the children a silk scarf. Have them move around the room as if they are light scarves fluttering and floating on the breeze. Suggest that the floating scarves become floating ghosts.

Ghost Movements
Halloween is coming and it's time for all good ghosts to practice their tricks: sneaking behind furniture, floating through walls, sliding under doors, darting in and out, jumping out with a "boo!" to surprise people. The children can take turns performing different tricks, or perform all the tricks together.

Dancing Ghosts

In ancient times, according to legend, everyone — including ghosts and other supernatural beings — came out to dance on Halloween. Have your children pretend to be ghosts with long white robes. Can they imagine how ghosts might have danced? Can they perform a sneaky dance, a funny dance, a fast dance?

Song: "Friendly Ghost"
(Sing to the tune of "Frere Jacque.")

I'm a friendly ghost
I'm a friendly ghost
Can't you see?
Can't you see?
The people that I greet
They turn white as a sheet
Just like me!
Just like me!

Other verses:
  I'm a scary ghost...
  I'm a funny ghost ...
  I'm a happy ghost...

Let each child decide what kind of ghost he or she would like to be. Everyone sings the song, filling in the chosen adjective, while the child acts out the kind of ghost described in the new verse.

Witches

Witches' Brew Warm-Up

Ancient stories describe how witches came out on Halloween and danced in a circle around their caldron, or pot of brew. Let your children hold hands and dance around an imaginary pot. Have them take turns stirring.

Witches' Dance

Describe how witches danced. Often two witches danced together, standing back-to-back and hooking their arms. They would kick up their heels and twirl around. Would your children like to pick partners and try this dance?

16

Song: "This Is the Way the Witches Dance"
(Sing to the tune of "Here We Go Round the Mulberry Bush.")

This is the way the witches dance,
Witches dance, witches dance
This is the way the witches dance
On Halloween night.

Other verses:
This is the way they kick their
heels...
This is the way they hook their
arms...
This is the way they turn
around...
(Repeat the first
verse.)

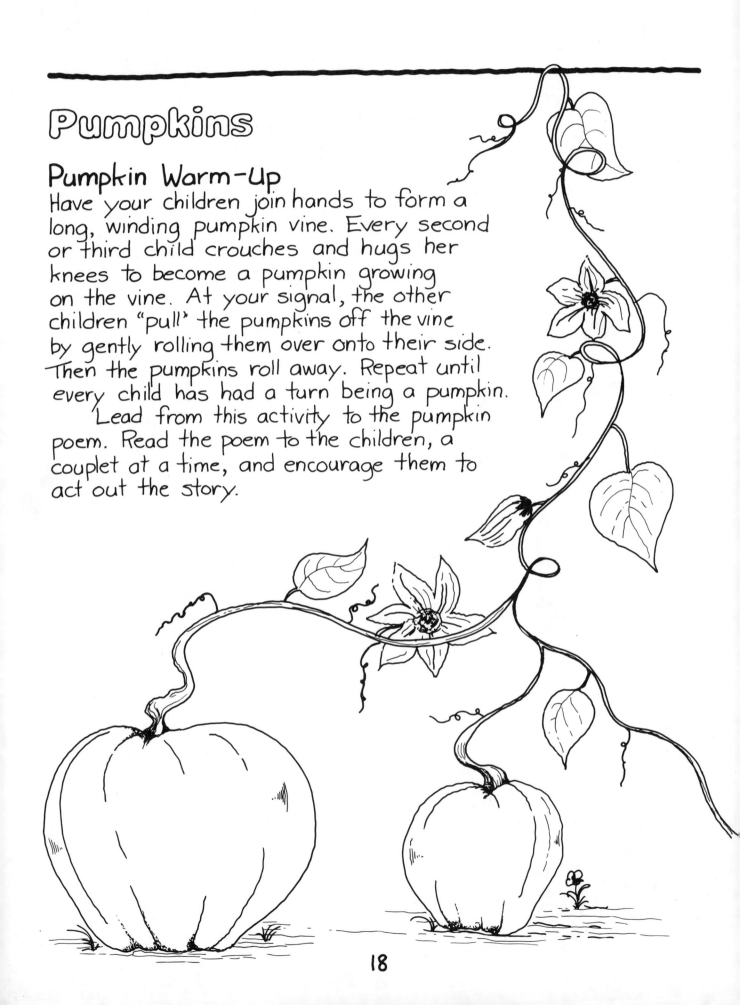

Pumpkins

Pumpkin Warm-Up

Have your children join hands to form a long, winding pumpkin vine. Every second or third child crouches and hugs her knees to become a pumpkin growing on the vine. At your signal, the other children "pull" the pumpkins off the vine by gently rolling them over onto their side. Then the pumpkins roll away. Repeat until every child has had a turn being a pumpkin.

Lead from this activity to the pumpkin poem. Read the poem to the children, a couplet at a time, and encourage them to act out the story.

Poem: "The Growing Pumpkin"

Early one morning as the sun popped out
A little white seed began to sprout.

It pushed its head up through the ground,
Waved its arms, and looked around.

At first the plant was very small
But then the plant began to sprawl.

It grew up the hill, to the very top
And there at last, it decided to stop.

Out popped a flower, a great big one
As gold as the color of the summer sun.

The plant was happy until one day
The beautiful flower fell away.

Then the plant grew sad, it felt real low
        Until a green ball started to grow.

        It grew and grew to a great
            big size
                Then turned bright
                orange—what a
                surprise!

Song: "Come and See the Pumpkin"
(Sing to the tune of "Did You Ever See a Lassie?")

Come and see the pumpkin, the pumpkin,
  the pumpkin
Come and see the pumpkin we picked from
  the patch.
We cleaned him and carved him
And cleaned him and carved him
Oh, come and see the pumpkin we picked
  from the patch.

Other verses:
  Come and see the pumpkin . . . with a
    candle inside...
  Come and see the pumpkin... with a big
    crooked grin...

Toys

Rag Doll Warm-Up

This is a good loosening-up exercise. Find or make a rag doll and show it to the children. Have them imagine that they are rag dolls; see if they can make their bodies go all limp. How would a rag doll move? Have them move each part of their bodies in a floppy fashion.

Story and Song: "Christmas Toys"

One Christmas Eve, Santa was getting ready to pack up all his toys. Before he put them into boxes, however, he decided to test them one last time. He took a small music box out of his pocket and opened the lid. It played a delightful tune. (Hum the tune to "Frère Jacque.")

First the music woke the ballerina doll. She got up and started to dance and sing. (Have the children dance and sing.)

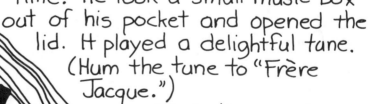

continued...

Story and Song: "Christmas Toys" continued

"I am dancing, I am dancing
'Round and 'round, 'round and 'round;
First I turn one way
Then I turn the other way
'Round and 'round, 'round and 'round."

Santa was pleased with the way she danced, so he wrapped her up and put her in his sack. Next a tin soldier got up and started marching to the music. (Have the children march and sing.)

"I am marching, I am marching
In a row, watch me go;
First I march one way
Then I march the other way
In a row, watch me go."

Next the model airplane woke, revved up its engines, and took off. Have your children fly and sing:

"I am flying, I am flying
'Round and 'round, up and down;
First I fly one way
Then I fly the other way
'Round and 'round, up and down."

Continue with other toys and movement verses until Santa's sack is quite full.

Other toys and verses:
electric train—"I am chugging—up and back, on a track...
puppet—"I am jerking—on a string, on a string...

Christmas Tree

Decorations Warm-Up

Show your children an assortment of tree decorations. Include some bulbs, tinsel, blinking lights, a string of popcorn, and an angel or star. Discuss the characteristics of each decoration, such as its shape and texture.

Pretend that you are dismayed to have so few decorations—hardly enough to decorate a tree. Then brighten up as you think of ways that the children can help you make some more. Here are some of the ways:

• Five children join hands in the center of a circle to make a five-pointed star. Have the children walk in a circle to make the star spin.

• All the children can become bulbs by rolling up into balls on the floor. Hooks can be fashioned by extending one arm and tipping the hand.

• The children stand up straight and tall like long strands of tinsel. Have them fall limply to the ground as someone "lets go" of them, or show them how to bend at the waist and hang their arms straight down as they are draped over a branch.

• Have the children spread their arms (the wires) and blink their eyes (the light bulbs) to show twinkling lights on a Christmas tree.

continued...

Decorations Warm-Up *continued*

• The children can move like angels by spreading their wings and flying around the room. At the end of their flight, the angels perch on top of a tree.

• Make some make-believe popcorn. First pretend to pour some oil into a giant skillet. Have all the children jump in and curl up like small kernels of corn. Turn on the heat and watch the children begin to squirm and wiggle as the pan gets hot. Soon they are rolling every which way to get away from the heat. Finally, they crouch on the balls of their feet, and when they can no longer stand the heat, they jump up with a loud "pop!"

   Have the children join hands to string the popcorn, then wrap themselves around an imaginary tree by moving in a spiral.

   Finally, the children can pretend to be trees and take turns decorating each other while they sing the song, "Here Stands a Lovely Christmas Tree."

Poem with Movements: "The Christmas Tree"

I went looking for a Christmas tree
    (cup hand over eye and begin walking)
I went to find one that would please me
The first tree I found was much too small
    (bend down and measure small tree
    with hand)
The second tree I found was much too tall
    (raise hands up high).
The third tree I found was much too thick
    (spread arms way out)
The fourth tree I found was thin as a stick
    (hold up one finger)
The fifth tree I found looked full and fine
    (outline a tree with your hands)
So I chopped it down and made it mine
    (swing imaginary axe to chop down tree)
I took it home and set it straight
And then began to decorate
    (pretend to hang ornaments)
When I was finished, I could see
That I had picked the perfect tree!

Song: "Here Stands a Lovely Christmas Tree"

(Sing to the tune of "Here We Go 'Round the Mulberry Bush.")

Here stands a lovely Christmas tree,
Christmas tree, Christmas tree.
Here stands a lovely Christmas tree
So early in the morning.

Other verses:
　　Here's a star for the Christmas tree...
　　Here are the lights for the Christmas
　　　　tree...
　　Here are some bulbs for the Christmas
　　　　tree...
　　Here's tinsel to hang on the Christmas
　　　　tree...
　　Put presents under the Christmas tree...

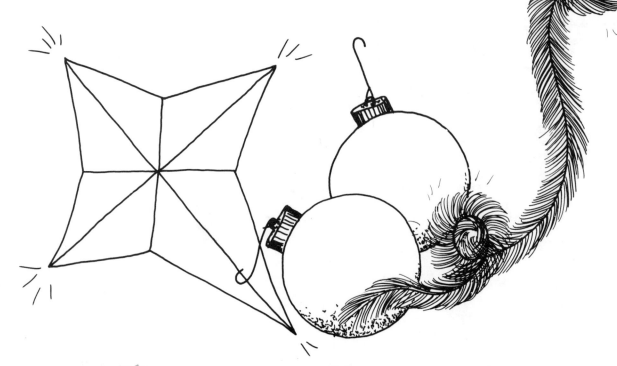

Reindeer

Running Warm Ups

Young children love to run. See if you can direct some of their natural pleasure into a movement exercise. Discuss the many different ways that people and animals can run. Let the children experiment with each of these suggested ways: fast, slow, backwards, in slow motion, in place, in a circle, on tip-toes, side-by-side with a friend, dashing in a race, with giant strides, with baby steps, like a deer, like a mouse, like a bear, like a monster, like a penguin, like a thief, down a hill, up a hill, in water, in snow, on hot cement.

Santa's Team

Each year before Christmas, Santa's reindeer have to get in shape for their long trip delivering toys. Only the fastest, strongest, and most agile will be able to make such a long, hard trip. Here are the things the reindeer practice: running fast, darting quickly in and out of places, leaping across roof tops, and landing gently so as not to wake anyone.

Have your children pretend they are reindeer getting in shape for Christmas. A fun prop for this activity is a string of several small bells tied onto the wrist or ankle of each child.

Poem: "Reindeer, Reindeer"

Reindeer, reindeer, jump up high
Reindeer, reindeer, across the sky
Reindeer, reindeer, land softly on the
   roofs
Reindeer, reindeer, step lightly with
   your hooves
Reindeer, reindeer, turn around
Reindeer, reindeer, touch the ground
Reindeer, reindeer, now run slow
Reindeer, reindeer, still far to go
Reindeer, reindeer, now run fast
Reindeer, reindeer, home at last!

Snow and Ice

Shiver Warm-Up

This activity will help your children warm-up on a cold day. Pretend you are controlling the heat in the room. Tell the children you are going to turn the heat down to make them all shiver. When their bodies are all shaking in the make-believe cold, turn the heat back up so their shivers gradually stop. Continue turning the heat up and down. The lower you turn the heat, the harder the children should shiver. Finally, turn the heat off altogether so that they "freeze" in position.

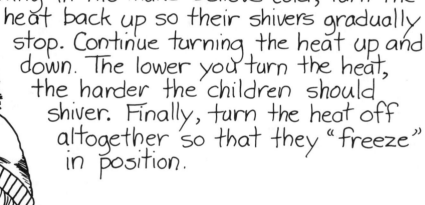

Skating

You and your children can pretend to join some winter skaters, skating on a frozen pond. Let the children skate around the room. Some cornmeal sprinkled on the floor will help them slide. Have the children take off their shoes and put on their make—believe skates. Play some waltz music and have the skaters glide in time to the music.

Song: "Snowflakes"
(Sing to the tune of "Twinkle, Twinkle, Little Star.")

Snowflakes, snowflakes, dance around
Snowflakes, snowflakes, touch the
   ground

Snowflakes, snowflakes, in the air
Snowflakes, snowflakes, everywhere

Snowflakes, snowflakes, dance around
Snowflakes, snowflakes, touch the
   ground

Snowmen

Snowball Warm-Up

Have the children lay on the floor, stretch out, and form a blanket of snow. Then have them pretend that other children are rolling them up to make large snowballs. The children roll across the floor, finally becoming so large they have to stand up and become jolly snowmen.

Melt-Down Warm-Up

Snowmen are frozen and must stand rigid all day and night. One day the sun shines so long and so brightly that the snowmen begin to thaw. Call out body parts, starting at the head and working down to the toes. The children begin moving these body parts slowly. As the day continues to get warmer, the snowmen gradually melt away. Have the children slowly and gracefully melt to the floor.

Song: "The Snowman"
(Sing to the tune of "The Muffin Man.")

Have you seen the snowman,
the snowman, the snowman
Have you seen the snowman
that lives in our front yard?

He has two brown potato eyes,
potato eyes, potato eyes
He has two brown potato eyes
and lives in our front yard.

Other verses:
   He has a big black top hat...
   He has an orange carrot nose...
   He has a long red woolen scarf...
   He has a great big smiley face...

Song: "Dance Around the Snowman"
(Sing to the tune of "Here We Go 'Round
the Mulberry Bush.")

This is the way we dance around,
dance around, dance around
This is the way we dance around
our snowman in the morning.

Actions for other verses: skip, hop, spin,
trot, crawl, sneak.

Song: "The Snowman Skipped Away"
(Sing to the tune of "Row, Row, Row Your Boat.")

The snow, snow, snowman
Came out-of-doors to play.
But the children cried, "Get back inside!
The sun is out today."

The snow, snow, snowman
Started to skip away.
But as he skipped his body dripped
Until a puddle lay.

Shadows

Shadow Warm-Up

Position a bright light to shine on you so that it casts your shadow on a wall. Show your children what a clever shadow you have — how it does everything you do. Show them how you can make your shadow wave, dance, twirl, and even fall down. Let the children take turns performing with their own shadows. Individually, or as a group, they might like to sing the "Shadow Song" as they perform.

Shadow Partners

Extend the individual warm-up activity into a partner activity. Have the children choose partners and take turns being each other's shadow. The children face one another. One child moves slowly while the other one — the shadow — tries to mirror what the first child is doing. After a few minutes, the children switch roles.

Mr. Groundhog

Legend has it that on February 2, Mr. Groundhog wakes up from his long winter's nap and goes outside. If he sees his shadow, he is frightened and runs back inside his hole to sleep for another six weeks. If he does not see his shadow, he stays outside to play, indicating that spring has arrived early.

Let your children take turns being Mr. Groundhog popping up out of his hole—a large cardboard box—while everyone else recites the poem, "Groundhog, Can You Play?"

Poem: "Groundhog, Can You Play?"

Groundhog, groundhog popping up today.
Groundhog, groundhog, can you play?

If you see your shadow, run away!
If there is no shadow, you can play.

Groundhog, groundhog, popping up today
Groundhog, groundhog, can you play?

Song: "Shadow Song"
(Sing to the tune of "Skip to My Lou.")

Dance, dance, just like me
Dance, dance, just like me
Dance, dance, just like me
Little shadow, just like me.

Other verses:
    Raise your hand, just like me...
    Kick your foot, just like me...
    Bend way down, just like me...
    Flap your arms, just like me...

Poem: "Little Shadow"

There is a little shadow
That dances on my wall
Sometimes it's big and scary
Sometimes it's very small.

Sometimes it's oh so quiet
And doesn't move at all
Then other times it chases me
Or bounces like a ball.

I'd love to meet that shadow
Who dances in the night
But it always runs away
When I turn off the light.

Valentines

Sticky Story Warm-Up

The children pretend they are making valentines when someone opens the door and a gust of wind blows in, knocking over the glue and scattering all the Valentines. As the children try to pick them up, their feet stick to the floor and their hands stick to whatever they touch. Let the children develop the story through their actions. How might they manage to walk? What happens if they all become stuck together? How can they become unstuck?

glue

Delivering Valentines

Have your children pretend they are mail carriers delivering valentine cards and packages. How would they carry a huge box of candy? How would they deliver cards to someone who lives on top of a mountain? On an island? Underwater? In a treehouse? On the moon?

Song: "Here Is My Valentine"
(Sing to the tune of "Here We Go 'Round the Mulberry Bush.")

Here is my valentine
My valentine, my valentine
Here is my valentine
Just for you.

Here is my valentine
My valentine, my valentine
Here is my valentine
I am stuck on you!

Movements: Have the children go around in a circle, each child giving a valentine to the next person. The valentines are still sticky with glue, so everyone gets stuck together. When everyone in the circle is finally stuck together, ask the children to think of ways they can get unstuck. For example: Everyone can jump in the swimming pool; everyone can pull away real hard; the teacher or parent can cut the valentines apart; or everyone can wait until the glue dries, then tear the cards apart.

SPRING THEMES

Wind

Scarf Warm-Up

Give each child a silk or nylon scarf. First encourage them to experiment with the scarf. What can it do? Can you wrap it around you like a skirt and twirl? Can you make it disappear and reappear? Can you toss it up high? Can you run with your scarf tied over your shoulders? Can you make a flag blowing in the wind?

Have the scarves come to represent the wind. How does the wind blow softly? How does it blow more strongly? Can you make the wind blow into a wild storm?

Storm Winds

A hurricane has hit! Have your children move through the storm to an area of the room that you have designated to be a safe place. Until they reach the safe place, they might toss about in the wind, get drenched in torrents of rain, get knocked over by sudden gusts, and have their umbrellas blow away. An unexpected tornado may send some children spinning away.

Clouds in the Breeze

Tie scarves or streamers to the arms of one or two children who will be the wind. Ask the others to pretend they are clouds on a breezy day. As you describe what is happening to the wind and clouds, the children interpret accordingly: "The wind is soft and gentle and the clouds are floating lazily around. The wind is picking up now; the breeze is jerky. There are little gusts and the clouds bounce up and down. Now the wind grows wild and fierce. The clouds hurry across the sky, sometimes crashing into each other (better set up some crashing rules!). Now the wind lets down a little and sends the clouds lightly spinning. Finally, the wind dies down. The air is very still, and the clouds rest."

Poem: "I See the Wind"

I see the wind when the leaves dance by;
I see the wind when the clothes hang dry;
I see the wind when the trees bend low;
I see the wind when the flags all blow.

I see the wind when the kites fly high;
I see the wind when the clouds float by;
I see the wind when it blows your hair;
I see the wind most everywhere!

Song: "My Kite"
(Sing to the tune of "The Farmer in the Dell.")

My kite is up so high,
My kite is up so high,
Oh my, just watch it fly!
My kite is up so high.

My kite is falling down,
My kite is falling down,
Oh no, it's near the ground!
My kite is falling down.

The wind has caught my kite,
The wind has caught my kite,
What fun, I'm on the run!
The wind has caught my kite.

(Repeat first verse.)

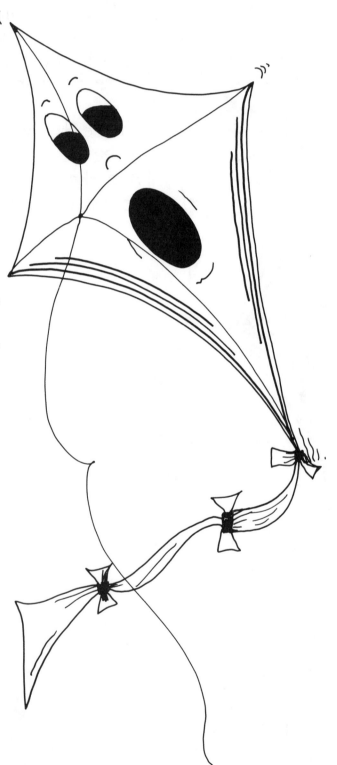

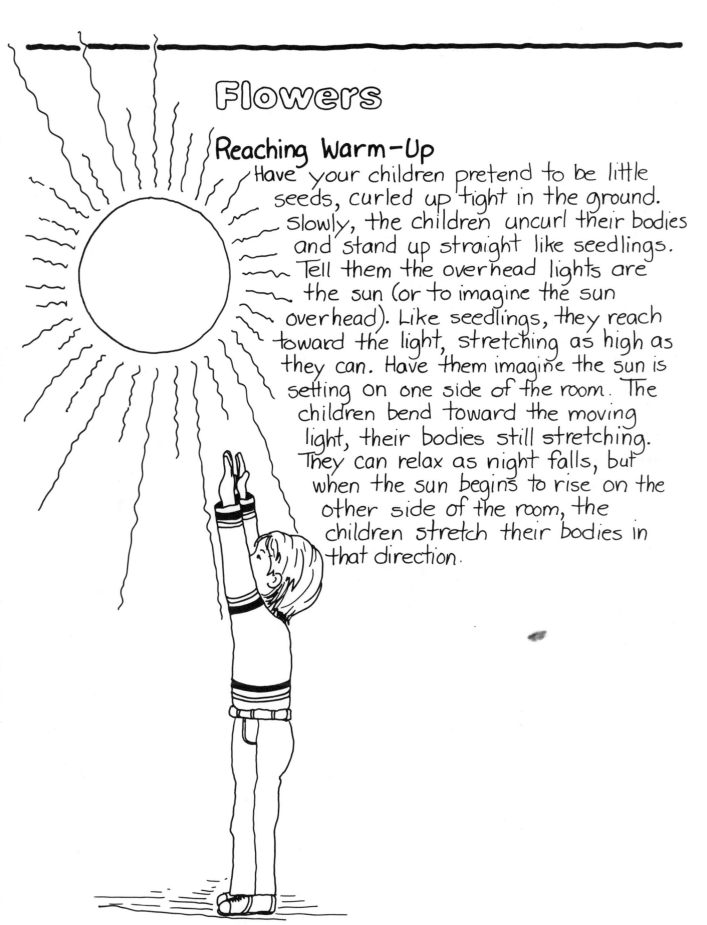

Flowers

Reaching Warm-Up

Have your children pretend to be little seeds, curled up tight in the ground. Slowly, the children uncurl their bodies and stand up straight like seedlings. Tell them the overhead lights are the sun (or to imagine the sun overhead). Like seedlings, they reach toward the light, stretching as high as they can. Have them imagine the sun is setting on one side of the room. The children bend toward the moving light, their bodies still stretching. They can relax as night falls, but when the sun begins to rise on the other side of the room, the children stretch their bodies in that direction.

Planting a Flower Garden

Your little gardners can pretend to use an assortment of tools for planting as they work through a gardening sequence. First have them dig a flower bed with a shovel. Next have them wheel over a load of fertilizer in a wheelbarrow. To make a wheelbarrow, the children can pair up, one lying belly-down on the floor and balancing on bent arms while her partner lifts her by the legs and propels her forward. The gardeners shovel in the fertilizer and work it into the soil with a hoe, then smooth it with a rake. They can either sow seeds, or poke them into the soil. Finally, they water their gardens with a watering can.

Song: "Help to Make My Garden"
(Sing to the tune of "Skip to My Lou.")

Sun in the sky, shine, shine, shine
Sun in the sky, shine, shine, shine
Sun in the sky, shine, shine, shine
Help to make my garden.

Other verses:
 Rain from the clouds, pour, pour, pour...
 Dirt in the ground, dig, dig, dig...
 Seeds in the dirt, grow, grow, grow...

Song: "When Springtime Is Here"
(Sing to the tune of "Here We Go 'Round the Mulberry Bush.")

This is the way we wake up and yawn
Wake up and yawn, wake up and yawn
This is the way we wake up and yawn
When springtime is here.

Other verses:
    This is the way we sprout our roots...
    This is the way we pop through the dirt...
    This is the way we stretch and grow...
    This is the way we shoot up so tall...
    This is the way we open our buds...
    This is the way we bend in the breeze...
    This is the way we smile at the sun...

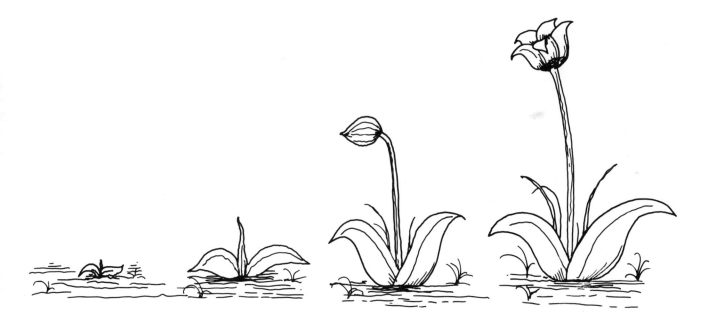

Honey Bees

Hive Warm-Up

Tell your children that the room is a beehive and that you are all honey bees. As the queen bee, you will assign tasks to your worker bees. Make up whimsical tasks that require large physical movements: for example, have some workers pour the pollen from flowers into pails, have others stir the pollen in a big pot to make honey, and have the rest sweep the hive. Before your busy bees have tired, appoint different children to take turns being the queen (or king) bee and to make up other imaginative jobs for the workers.

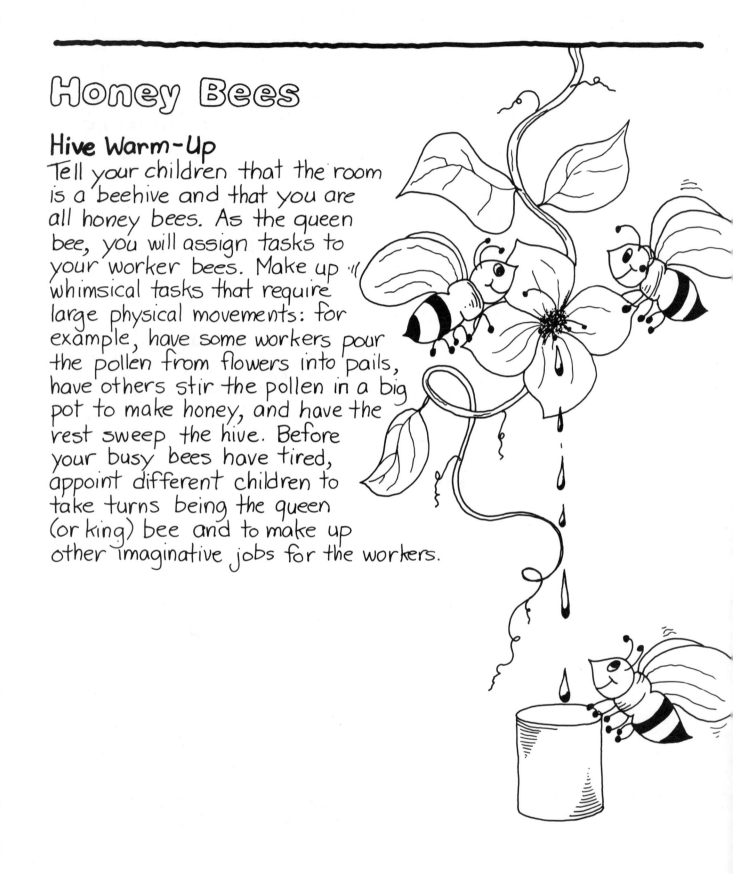

Story: "Dance of the Honey Bee"

One day a honey bee was out looking for flowers when he happened to find a hidden valley full of the most beautiful blossoms he had ever seen. He hurried home to get his friends, but by the time he reached the hive, he was too tired to fly back to the valley. Instead, he showed his friends how to find the flowers with a dance.

He flew in one direction, flapping his wings ten times to show how many miles. Then he stopped and flew around in a circle once to show that at this spot there were a few flowers. Next he flew off in a different direction, flapping his wings five times (for five miles), then stopped and circled the area many times to indicate that at this spot there were many flowers.

Let your children take turns being the bee and dancing the directions to the flowers. Technically, this is not the exact dance of the honey bee, but an "adaptation" that young children will enjoy more.

Poem: "The Tiny Bee"

Once there was a tiny bee
Small and fuzzy and hard to see.
"Oh, foo!" said the bee. "I wish I could stand
Taller than all throughout the land!"

And do you know what? Her wish came true.
She grew and grew and grew and grew.

"Oh, woe is me," said the giant bee,
"I cannot fly when I'm big as a tree'!"
And the flowers all wept when she came to call,
For she squashed their petals and made
    them fall.

"Oh, woe is me, what shall I do?
I'll wish again till my dream comes true."
And slowly, slowly, before her eyes,
She shrank back down to her regular size.

She soared up high and zoomed down low;
Now wherever she wanted, she could go.
The flowers all smiled as she flew by,
Happy to see their small friend in the sky.

"Oh, golly gee, it's fun to be
Small and light and free as a bee!"

Movements: Let your children expand
on the story if they wish, acting out
other situations the bee may have
encountered when she was big.

Bunnies

Jumping Warm-Up

Show the children a jack-in-the-box, or explain how one works. Then ask the children to be a jumping jack. Have them squat way down in their imaginary boxes; then, when the lid pops open, they jump up.

Can a jack-in-the-box jump in other ways? Have the children recite the "Jack-in-the-Box" poem as they act out other position words, for example, "**out** of the box," "**over** the box," or "**across** the room."

Animal Hop

Invite all jumping animals to an Animal Hop. Play some lively music as the children pretend to be a variety of animals that jump: Kangaroos, bunnies, frogs, crickets, fleas. Show them how to bend way down before they jump, spring up, then land again in a crouch.

The Bunny Trail

The bunny rabbits are in training so that they will be in shape to hop down the bunny trail and deliver baskets of eggs on Easter. Here are the kinds of hopping they must practice: fast, slow, backwards, high over tree stumps, low under fences, on one foot, and carefully while carrying a basketful of eggs.

Of course, your bunnies may prefer to run or skip down the bunny trail on Easter. Let each child decide how he or she would like to come down the trail. As the child performs the movement, have the others sing the song, "Down the Bunny Trail," singing the child's first name in the first blank, and the chosen movement in the second.

Song: "Down The Bunny Trail"
(Sing to the tune of "Here Comes Peter Cottontail.")

Here comes _____ Cottontail
_____ down the bunny trail
Hippety, hoppety, Easter's on its way!

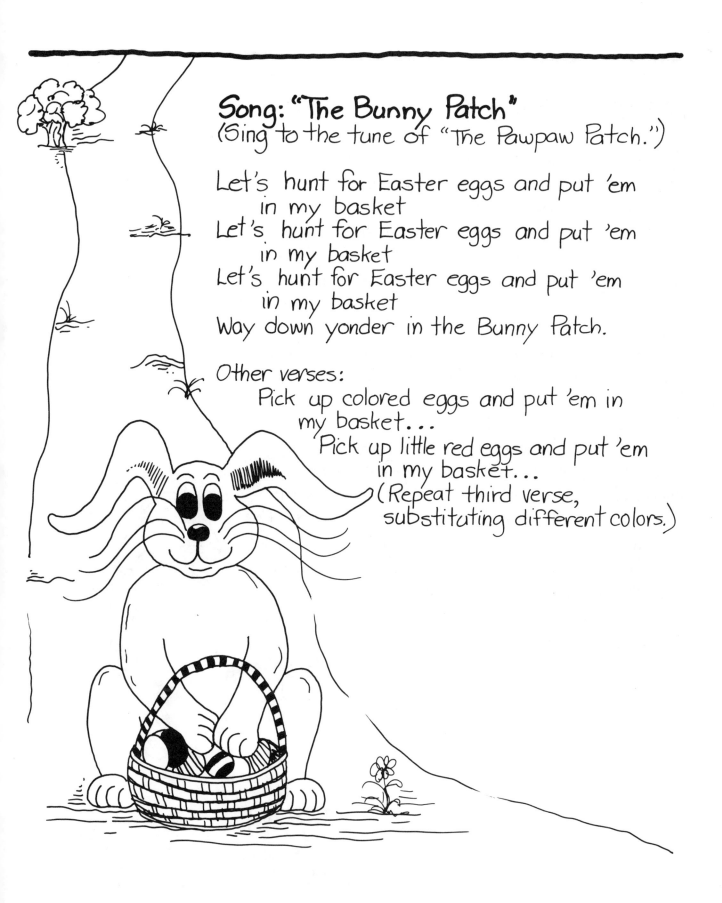

Song: "The Bunny Patch"
(Sing to the tune of "The Pawpaw Patch.")

Let's hunt for Easter eggs and put 'em
    in my basket
Let's hunt for Easter eggs and put 'em
    in my basket
Let's hunt for Easter eggs and put 'em
    in my basket
Way down yonder in the Bunny Patch.

Other verses:
    Pick up colored eggs and put 'em in
      my basket...
      Pick up little red eggs and put 'em
        in my basket...
        (Repeat third verse,
          substituting different colors.)

Butterflies

Caterpillar Warm-Up

Have your children get down in a crawling position and crawl in a line. Next, show them how to hook up by placing their hands on the back or legs of the child in front of them. Explain that each child is now a segment of one long caterpillar's body. Have the children all start crawling with the same leg. See if they can crawl all around the room in this fashion. Some rhythmic music will help the crawlers coordinate their movements.

Gradually lead the children into a dramatization of the butterfly story, which describes a caterpillar's metamorphosis. Provide brightly colored scarves that the children can hide in their hands and unfurl as the butterfly emerges from its cocoon.

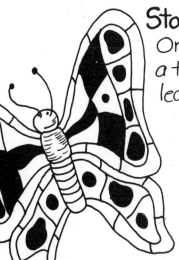

Story: "The Butterfly"

One warm day, a caterpillar crawled up into a tree for a nap in one of the cool green leaves. First she curled up on the leaf and spun a web around herself. In this cozy covering, she slept and slept.

When the caterpillar woke up, she chewed her way out of the cocoon. But suddenly she realized she no longer had her many legs. How would she ever get home?

The caterpillar started to cry. Then as she tried to wipe her tears, she discovered to her joy, that while asleep she had grown two beautiful butterfly wings. She opened her wings, flapped and flapped, and was soon soaring through the sky.

How would the story end? Where does the butterfly go and what happens to her? Ask the children to help you finish the story.

Song: "Grow Caterpillar"
(Sing to the tune of "Row, Row, Row Your Boat.")

Crawl, crawl, caterpillar; you're such a fuzzy sight
Don't you know, it's time to grow
So crawl with all your might.

Other verses:
    Spin, spin, caterpillar; spin your cocoon so tight...
    Wake, wake, caterpillar; break out into the light...
    Fly, fly, caterpillar; it's time for your first flight...

53

Birds

Wing Warm-Up

There is no prop that spurs the imagination more than a pair of wings. You can simply cut out a pair of wings and tape them to a child's wrists. Or you can construct a more permanent set out of a piece of fabric about 2/3 yard by 1-1/3 yards. Cut one-inch strips up from one long side, stopping two inches short of the opposite side. Mark the center on the side with the two-inch margin. About six inches from each side of this mark, sew on a pot holder ring, a loop of yarn or ribbon, or attach a curtain ring. A child places the fabric — the wing span — across her shoulders and holds it in place by hooking her thumbs in the hoops.

Let your children experiment with their wings as you recite the "Wings of a Bird" poem.

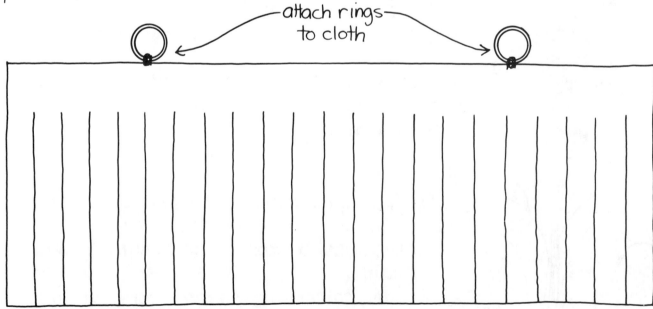

attach rings to cloth

Story: "Learning to Fly"

A mother bird has been sitting on her nest of eggs. One day the eggs hatch, and the mother bird busies herself with finding food and feeding her babies. At last she decides they are big enough to learn to fly. She flies around the nest and shows her babies how it is done. Soon all the little birds are flying but one, who is afraid. How can the mother bird get her baby to fly?

Have your children come up with possible solutions, for example, "by pushing the baby out of the nest," "by sending up a sneaky cat to scare the baby into flying away," or "by having two other birds hold onto the baby's wings to help him fly." Encourage the children to retell the story with the agreed-upon ending, acting out as many elements of the story as they can (pecking their way out of an egg, flapping their baby wings, and so on).

Poem: "Wings of a Bird"

Flying fast, flying slow
Soaring high, swooping low
Swirling and twirling, and gliding through
   the air
The wings of a bird travel everywhere.

Poem: "Four Little Birdies"

Four little birdies high in the tree
One flew away, then there were three.

Three little birdies with feathers so new
One flew away, then there were two.

Two little birdies out in the sun
One flew away, then there was one.

One little birdie alone in the nest
Afraid to fly out and join the rest.

Come little birdie, come fly like me
Come little birdie, fly out of the tree.

Flap your wings, flap your wings down
So you can fly over field and town.

Up, up and away the birdie did fly
Up over the trees, up into the sky.

Four little birdies now up so high
I almost forgot to wave them "Goodbye!"

56

Playground

Bouncing Balls Warm-Up

For this fun warm-up activity, your children pretend that they have accidently swallowed a rubber bouncing ball. Have them dramatize what might happen as the ball moves inside their bodies, first into a shoulder, then to an elbow, stomach, knee or foot. Play some bouncy music to which the balls inside the children can keep time.

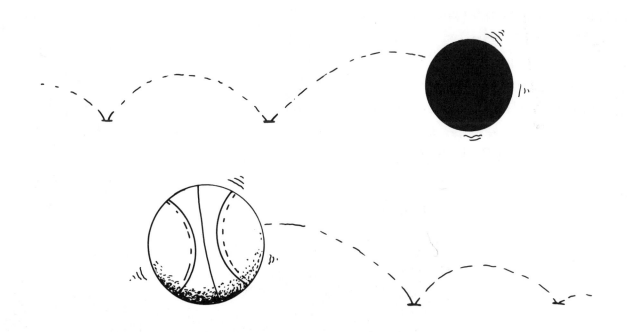

Playground Equipment

Invite your children to help build an imaginary playground on an empty lot. Ask them to name some equipment they would like to have, then help them figure out ways to use their bodies to make the items. Here are some examples:

- Swings. The children can each make a swing by swinging their arms parallel at their sides (like the chains or ropes of a swing). Or two children can face each other and hold hands to form a swing. A teddy bear or a doll might enjoy a ride in this cooperative swing.

- Tunnel. Several children line up, then bend over and put their hands on the ground to form a tunnel. The others crawl through.

- See-Saw. Keeping their bodies straight, the children spread their arms and move them up and down like a see-saw.

- Spring Horse (or other animal). The children, elbows bent, pretend to hold the posts at either side of the animal's head as they bob up and down by bending their knees or jumping in place.

- Sliding board. The children sit on the floor with legs extended, then bend their knees and bring up their legs to form an incline. A doll or stuffed toy can slide down the incline.

- Basketball Hoop. This one's easy — the children form a wide circle in front of themselves with their arms. They can take turns tossing foam balls or wads of paper into each other's basket.

Song: "Playground Play"
(Sing to the tune of "Row, Row, Row Your Boat.")

Pump, pump, pump the swing
Pump as high as you can;
You pump so high
You touch the sky
Then down you come again.

Climb, climb, climb the bars
As many as you can;
You climb to the top
And then you stop
Then down you climb again.

Ride, ride, ride your trike
Ride as fast as you can;
All the way 'round
The whole playground
Then around you go again.

Water

Water Warm-Up

Come on in, the water's fine! Help your children get in the mood for some water fun. First ask how many different ways to swim they can think of. Next, have them imagine how they might move if they were in water up to their ankles. How would they move in water up to their waists? Up to their necks?

Pass out imaginary water masks and have your children slip them on and dive under water. What do they see? As they stroke through the water with their arms, have the children take turns naming something that they might see underwater, for example, fish, tall waving plants, sharks, crabs. Half of the children can be tall waving plants while the other half swim carefully between them.

Water Cycle

Ask your children to imagine they are raindrops that have just fallen. Have them rotate slowly around the room, joining hands with a raindrop next to them to become a small stream. The streams continue to rotate, each connecting with another stream to form a river. The rivers move faster and faster, cascading over large rocks. The children move with more speed and bumpier motions, their heads, arms and knees bending up and down to show the current.

As they pass a designated spot, the children turn into whirlpools, forming small four-person circles and twirling about. Eventually the children all hold hands and flow into the ocean, forming one large circle. Have the children slowly come together with arms raised, then flow backwards with graceful arm movements to represent the tides.

As the sun shines over the ocean, the children once again become drops of water that rise back up into the sky to form rain clouds.

Crossing a River

There are many ways to cross a river—let your children act out some. They can step and hop across over stones if the river is shallow; jump across if it's narrow; row a boat or paddle a canoe if it's deep; and swim across if they can, practicing different strokes as they sing the song, "Swimming, Swimming."

Song: "Swimming, Swimming"
(Sing to the tune of "Sailing, Sailing.")

Swimming, swimming, over the ocean blue
I love to dive, I love to kick
How about you?

Side stroke, back float—underwater, too
Swimming is so much fun
It's what I love to do!

Bubbles

Bubble Warm-Up

Blow some bubbles with a wand and soap solution so your children can see what they are like and how they move. Then bring out a large hula hoop. This will be a giant wand. As you slowly wave the wand, have the children run through the hoop, emerging as beautiful bubbles. Let the children float around the room awhile, eventually settling down to the ground with a gentle pop.

Magic Bubble Rides

Have your children pretend to crawl inside a magic bubble that can take them wherever they want to go. Perhaps they'll want to roll and bob about over the ocean, fizz with the other bubbles in a bottle of soda, sit on the back of an elephant for a ride through the jungle, or perch on the wing of an airplane as it soars through the sky.
Encourage the children to act out different situations where their bubbles might take them.

Song: "Blowing Bubbles"
(Sing to the tune of "I'm Forever Blowing Bubbles.")

I'm forever blowing bubbles
Pretty bubbles in the air
They fly so high
Nearly reach the sky
But then they fall
And fade and die.
Bubbles I keep blowing
Blowing here and there
I'm forever blowing bubbles
Pretty bubbles in the air.

Song: "My Bubble Flew Over the Ocean"

(Sing to the tune of "My Bonnie Lies Over the Ocean.")

My bubble flew over the ocean
My bubble flew over the sea
My bubble over the rainbow
Oh, come back my bubble to me!

Come back, come back,
Oh, come back my bubble
   to me, to me
Come back, come back,
Oh, come back my bubble
   to me!

The Circus

Ring Warm-Up

Every circus has a ring in which the circus people perform their acts. Ask your children to help you make a big ring. A ring, of course, is a circle. So first have the children hold their arms out and turn little circles with their fingers, then bigger circles with their arms. Have the children spin around in circles. When they have exhausted ideas for making circles by themselves, suggest that they join hands and step back to make one gigantic circle, or ring, for the circus.

Circus Acts

Let your children take turns being the ring master and introducing the different circus acts. Here are some performance possibilities:

- Stepping horses. The children pretend to be prancing horses with decorated saddles, or the people who ride the horses bareback and perform tricks in the saddle.
- Elephant Walk. The elephants walk heavily in a line, hooking their trunks (right hands) to the tails (left hands) of the elephant standing directly in front of them. Or the elephant can perform by themselves on a balance beam, walk across carefully, swinging their long trunks (bodies bent over so extended arms with hands clasped can swing from side to side).
- Tightrope. Children can step very carefully with their arms held out on either side for balance.
- Acrobats. The children can show off their somersaults, headstands, cartwheels, splits, or other acrobatic tricks.
- Clowns. The children can do silly things, like run and fall, wiggle, jump, and trip each other (if they're performing on grass or carpeting).

Song: "Tightrope Walkers Balancing"
(Sing to the tune of "Mary Had a Little Lamb.")

Tightrope walkers balancing
Balancing, balancing
Tightrope walkers balancing
On a stretch of string.

Elephants are walking slow
Walking slow, walking slow
Elephants are walking slow
In a line they go.

Bareback riders prance along
Prance along, prance along
Bareback riders prance along
While they sing this song.

Balloons

Balloon Warm-Up

Let your children observe you blow up
a real balloon. How does the balloon
look before it's blown up? Afterward? What
happens when you let the air out?

      Have the children pretend to be limp
balloons. As you pretend to blow them up,
they expand, thrusting out their chests
and opening their arms. After they
have floated about lightly, let them pop
each other with a finger so they deflate
quickly. Deflating can be a
little crazy with a large group.
In this case, suggest that the
children stand in a circle as
they inflate so they can rush
backwards without crashing
into each other as they deflate.
If the children have been holding
their breaths as they inflate,
the sound effects are great
as they deflate.

Balloon Poppers

Have the children pretend to blow up enough balloons to fill the room. Then the children each decide for themselves where to tape a long sharp pin (make-believe, of course) on some part of their body — the knee, toe, elbow, nose, or hip for example. Set the balloon poppers loose on the balloons. They'll have to reach very low to get all the balloons in the room, no matter where their poppers are. Great exercise!

Song: "Blow, Blow, Blow Your Balloon"
(Sing to the tune of "Row, Row, Row Your Boat.")

Grab, grab, grab a balloon
Give it a big blow,
The more you fill it up with air
The bigger it will grow.

Blow, blow, blow your balloon
Perhaps now you should stop;
For if you blow it up too much
It will surely pop!

Feet

Bare Feet Warm-Up

Children love to play in their bare feet, so these warm-ups will be naturals. First have the children sit on the floor and concentrate on their feet, rubbing them against each other, wiggling their toes, knocking their big toes together, bobbing their heels, bending their knees and stamping.

Now have them stand up and make their feet behave in different ways. Can they be quiet feet, sneaky feet, heavy feet, tiny feet, slow feet, clumsy feet? Can the feet walk, run, skip, march, and jump?

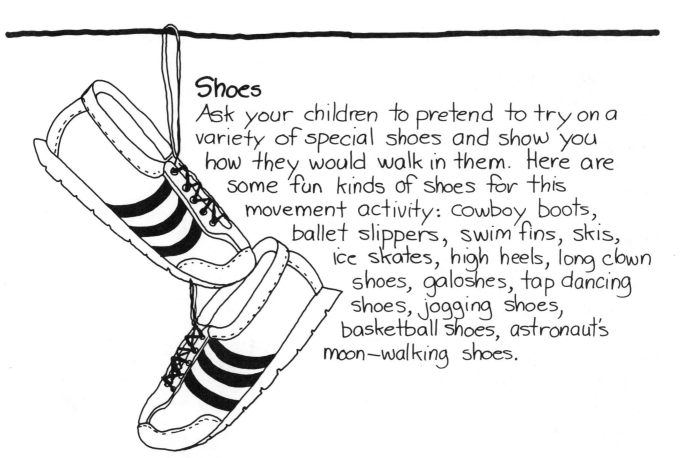

Shoes

Ask your children to pretend to try on a variety of special shoes and show you how they would walk in them. Here are some fun kinds of shoes for this movement activity: cowboy boots, ballet slippers, swim fins, skis, ice skates, high heels, long clown shoes, galoshes, tap dancing shoes, jogging shoes, basketball shoes, astronaut's moon-walking shoes.

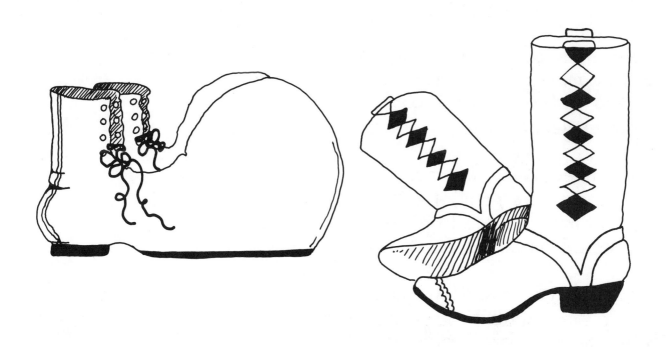

Poem "Magic Feet"

One day I found a pair of shoes
Out upon the walk
They looked like any other shoes
Except this pair could talk!

They told me they were special shoes
That I might wear that day
I quickly slipped them on my feet
And headed out to play.

When I ran with all my friends
My shoes they went so fast
I found myself out in the lead
Instead of near the last.

And when we started jumping
Over brooks and streams
My feet just seemed to fly across
Like they do in dreams.

I wore my shoes in swimming
And swam across the lake
I looked just like a motor boat
And even left a wake.

Next I tried some dancing
The shoes were really neat
They let me spin and leap and bend
And never missed a beat.

What a special day that was
What a special treat
To be the best at everything
To have two magic feet!

74

Song: "Have You Seen My Feet?"
(Sing to the tune of "Have You Seen the Muffin Man?")

Have you seen my dancing feet
My dancing feet, my dancing feet
Have you seen my dancing feet
As they dance on down the street?

Sometimes fast, sometimes slow
Sometimes high, sometimes low
Have you seen my dancing feet
As they dance on down the street?

Other verses:
    Have you seen my running feet...
    Have you seen my jumping feet...
    (Substitute other movements the children
    want to perform.)

Rabbit and Turtle

Fast and Slow Warm-Up

Discuss the concepts of fast and slow with your children. Ask them to name things that go fast—jet planes, race cars, runners, and so on. Then ask them to name things that go slow—snails, turtles, trucks uphill, and so on. Have the children talk slowly, then fast; walk slowly, then fast.

Have the children form a circle and walk around slowly, then as fast as they can without bumping into each other. Next try dancing slowly to slow music, then fast to fast music. If you have a three-speed record player, put on a 45-speed record. Tell the children to walk around in a circle to the rhythm of the music. First play the record at normal speed (45 rpm). Then change the speed to 78 rpm (very fast), and then to 33-1/3 rpm (very slow). The children enjoy this activity because the record sounds so funny played at the wrong speeds.

Story: "Rabbit and Turtle"

One day Rabbit asked Turtle if he would like to race to town and back. Turtle said, "Okay," and started slowly down the road.

Rabbit laughed as he hopped past Turtle. "Turtle is so slow, I will win easily!" he bragged.

When he reached town, Rabbit noticed a carnival. "Oh, I love carnival rides," said Rabbit. "Surely I have time to go on a few rides before I start back to the forest." So Rabbit went on some rides (let the children decide which rides and act them out). He had such a good time, he forgot about the time—and the race.

It was night when Rabbit suddenly remembered the race. He hurried back to the forest. But it didn't matter how fast he ran now, for just as it was getting dark, Turtle had slowly reached the forest and won the race.

Song: "The Rabbit and the Turtle"

(Sing to the tune of "The Farmer in the Dell.")

The rabbit ran so fast
The rabbit ran so fast
Heigh-ho the derry-o
The rabbit ran so fast.

Other verses:
    The turtle ran so slow...
    The rabbit stopped to play...
    The turtle won that day...

Wheels

Travel Warm-Up

Pretend you are going on a trip. Begin on bicycles, showing the children how to lie on their backs and pedal with their legs. While you are pedaling, the children can decide exactly where they want to go.

Suddenly you hear a train. Now the children can hop aboard, making their arms move back and forth like wheels on a train. Hook together to form one long train by having the children line up and place their left hands on the shoulder of the person in front of them while continuing to rotate their right hands like train wheels.

When the children tire of the train, toot the whistle and call "All out for _____!" (wherever they have decided to go). For the return trip, recommend they take a plane to make the trip short. After they have zoomed around the room, their radar signals working to prevent any mid-air collisions, the children can circle the airfield, drop their landing gear, and take turns landing.

Body Wheels

How many ways can your children make wheels with their bodies? Can they make their heads turn like wheels? Their arms, hands, fingers, hips, legs, feet? Can they make more than one body wheel move at a time? In different directions?

Have the children pair up and coordinate their bodies in some way to make a machine that runs on wheels — as many wheels as possible. As a grand finale, have all the children come together and create one giant machine made up of many wheels and moving parts. All the wheels can work together simultaneously, or one wheel can begin turning, activate the next wheel, and so on until all the wheels are turning. As the last wheel turns, the machine can "Bong!" and wind down by having the wheels slow down and stop in reverse order.

Song: "Off We Go"
(Sing to the tune of "Frère Jacques.")

Here's the train, here's the train
  All aboard, all aboard
    Chug-a-chug-a-choo-choo
    Chug-a-chug-a-choo-choo
    Off we go, off we go.

Other verses:
    Here's the airplane...
        chug-a-chug-a-zoom-zoom...
    Here's the boat...
        chug-a-chug-a-toot-toot...

Song: "Old MacDonald Built a Car"
(Sing to the tune of "Old MacDonald Had a Farm.")

Old MacDonald built a car
E-I-E-I-O
And on this car he put some wheels
E-I-E-I-O
With a wheel here, and a wheel there
Here a wheel, there a wheel
Everywhere a wheel, wheel
Old MacDonald built a car
E-I-E-I-O

Other verses:
    Old MacDonald built a clock . . .
    Old MacDonald built an engine...

Song: "Wheels Turning"
(Sing to the tune of "Frère Jacques.")

I am moving, I am moving
See me turn, see me turn
First I turn one way
Then I turn the other way
See me turn, see me turn.